I0798712

Ned Rorem

Water Music

BOOSEY & HAWKES

AN IMAGEM COMPANY

DISTRIBUTED BY

HAL•LEONARD®
CORPORATION

7777 W. BLUEMOUND RD. P.O. BOX 13819 MILWAUKEE, WI 53213

Water Music was first performed April 9, 1967, by California's Oakland Youth Orchestra, conducted by Robert Hughes, with soloists Thomas Halpin, violin, and Larry London, clarinet.

Instrumentation

Solo B♭ Clarinet
Solo Violin

Flute
(doubling Piccolo)

Oboe
(doubling English Horn)

Bassoon

Horn in F

*Percussion

Harp

Piano
(doubling Celesta)

Strings

*Vibraphone, Glockenspiel, Triangle, Gong, Bongos (2), Cymbals, Snare Drum, Bass Drum, Tenor Drum

Duration: 17 minutes

Orchestral material available on rental by direct application to:

BOOSEY & HAWKES, INC.
30 West 57th Street
New York, N. Y. 10019

Most composers hate to whistle in the dark. They like to work toward deadlines, on well-defined projects. Hence their sometimes hopeless periods — periods of mourning what is commonly called inspiration — can be suddenly relieved at receiving a realistic demand. Such was my case during the sterile spring of 1966 when Robert Hughes offered me a carefully specified commission. He also set the date for its premiere, and I set promptly to work, fertile now with the inspiration of Hughes' practical needs.

The stars of his Youth Orchestra were a violinist and a clarinetist, still in high school but already thoroughly professional performers (though neither planned on a musical career). Hughes suggested, since there existed no major concertante piece featuring this combination, that I write seventeen minutes of music outlining brilliant and hard parts for these two soloists, accompanied by an orchestration equally brilliant but less hard. He then detailed for me the many accomplishments and few weaknesses of his other young players.

From these delimitations flowed some WATER MUSIC, mostly conceived, appropriately enough, in Saratoga Springs during November 1966. From a mulling of the given stylistic sonorities there naturally evolved a Concerto Grosso wherein not only the soloists but each section of the orchestra were given opportunities to illustrate themselves. Simultaneously the formal pattern grew into a Theme and Variations, standard, except that the unadorned theme — here called the *Tune* — is introduced after the first of the nine variants.

Like most programmatic titles, this one was tacked on after the fact, less because water had impelled me, or because I wished to recall Handel, than because names like Concerto Grosso seemed too literally dry for my sort of music. But if my own images herein are not necessarily aquatic, I won't discourage your freedom to "see" whatever you choose in the sounds.

The sounds, in addition to those of the principles, are made by 1 Flute (interchangeable with Piccolo), 1 Oboe (interchangeable with English Horn), 1 Bassoon, 1 French Horn, 2 Percussion Players (playing cymbals, gongs, bongos, vibraphone and a few other things — but no timpani), a Harp, a Piano (interchangeable with Celesta) and the usual strings.

The formal sequence is as follows:

Prologue (Variation 1) — Nervous
The Tune — Calm and Sad
Variation 2 — Faster
Variation 3 — Quite Fast
Variation 4 — Lifeless, Slow
Variation 5 — Ugly, blurred, white expressionless, cold non-vibrato, molto portamento, and out of tune
Variation 6 — Cold and Strange
Variation 7 — Gently
Variation 8 — Fast
Variation 9 — Calm

Ned Rorem

WATER MUSIC

NED ROREM

Printed in U.S.A.

5
SOLO
Clar.
Vln.
10
Fl.
E.H.
Bsn.
Hn.
Bng.
Hp.
Pno.
(2)
molto
(ff sempre)
Vla.
Cello
Bass
unis.

15
Fl.
E.H.
Bsn.
Hn.
Gong
Bng.
Hp.
Pno.
SOLO
Clar.
Vln.
Vln. 1
Vln. 2
Vla.
Cello
Bass
sfz
f
ff
(1)
[C♮]
tr
7
6

20
SOLO Clar.
SOLO Vln.
25
Fl.
E.H.
Change to Oboe
p
molto
sfz
Bsn.
Hn.
S. D.
tr
Cym.
sock
B. D.
Hp.
[B♭]
ff
Pno.
gliss.
Vln. 1
Vln. 2
mutes
arco
Vla.
Cello
pizz.
Bass

Hp.
S O L O
Clar.
Vln.
30
[F♮]
35
molto rit.
[E♭]
molto rit.
f
mf

THE TUNE:
CALM and SAD (♩= 54)
40
Fl.
Ob.
Bsn.
Hn.
p
poco
(like a distant tint rather than a "voice")
molto vibrato
Vibr.
p legato
poco
Hp.
p
[E♮]
Pno.
SOLO Clar.
mp espr.
mf
SOLO Vln.
mp espr.
mf
THE TUNE:
CALM and SAD (♩= 54)
40
Vln. 1
Vln. 2
mutes
arco
p
poco
Vla.
mutes
p
poco
Cello
mutes
p
poco
Bass
mutes
(pizz.)
p

45
Fl.
Ob.
Bsn.
Hn.
Vibr.
Hp.
[A♭]
[B♮]
Pno.
SOLO
Clar.
Vln.
mp
mp
45
Vln.
1
2
Vla.
Cello
Bass

50
Fl.
Ob.
Bsn.
Hn.
mp
Vibr.
Hp.
[B♭ E♭]
[E♮ A♮]
Pno.
SOLO
Clar.
p
pp
Vln.
p
pp
50
arco
1
Vln.
2
p espr.
mutes off
Vla.
Cello
Bass

55 VARIATION 2
FASTER (♩= 92)
Fl.
Ob.
Oboe
Bsn.
Hn.
Bng.
S.D.
B.D.
Hp.
Pno.
[To Celesta]
SOLO Clar.
SOLO Vln.
55 VARIATION 2
FASTER (♩= 92)
Vln. 1
Vln. 2
mutes off
pizz.
Vla.
Cello
Bass

60
Fl.
Ob.
Bsn.
Hn.
Bng.
S.D.
B.D.
Hp.
Cel.
Celesta
SOLO
Clar.
Vln.
60
1
Vln.
2
pizz.
pizz.
Vla.
Cello
Bass

Fl.
Ob.
Bsn.
Hn.
Bng.
S.D.
B.D.
Hp.
Cel.
S
O
L
O
Clar.
Vln.
65
Vln.
1
2
Vla.
Cello
Bass
(non div.)
(non div.)
65

Fl.
Ob.
Bsn.
Hn.
Bng.
S. D.
B. D.
gliss.
[C♯]
Hp.
Cel.
SOLO Clar.
SOLO Vln.
arco
div.
unis.
1
Vln.
2
Vla.
Cello
Bass

70
Fl.
Ob.
Bsn.
Hn.
Bng.
Tri.
S.D.
B.D.
Hp.
[B♮]
Cel.
SOLO Clar.
Vln.
pizz.
arco
70
div.
pizz.
1
Vln.
2
Vla.
Cello
Bass

Fl.
Ob.
Bsn.
Hn.
Bng.
S.D.
B.D.
Hp.
[G♭]
[G♮ A♭]
Cel.
SOLO
Clar.
Vln.
1
Vln.
2
Vla.
Cello
Bass
unis.
unis.
arco
(pizz.)
f
ff
mf

75
Fl.
Ob.
Bsn.
Hn.
Bng.
Tri.
S.D.
B.D.
Hp.
[C♮A♮]
Cel.
To Piano
SOLO
Clar.
Vln.
pizz.
Vln. 1
Vln. 2
unis.
Vla.
Cello
div.
Bass
80
arco, trem.

VARIATION 3
QUITE FAST (♩. = ♩ = 80)
Fl.
Ob.
Bsn.
Hn.
Hp.
12/8 (4/4) ♩. = ♩ = 80
Pno.
Piano
S O L O Clar.
Vln.
VARIATION 3
QUITE FAST (♩. = ♩ = 80)
arco
Vln. 1 2
Vla.
div.
fp sub.
Cello
(pizz.)
Bass

85
Fl.
Ob.
Bsn.
Hn.
Hp.
[F♯ G♯ E♭]
f
gliss.
8
Pno.
ff
sf
SOLO
Clar.
Vln.
85
Vln.
1
2
Vla.
fp
mf
Cello
Bass.

90
Fl.
Ob.
Bsn.
Hn.
Tri.
Hp.
[F♮B♭A♭D♭C♭]
[D♮F♭]
[F♮D♭G♭]
Pno.
SOLO
Clar.
Vln.
90
1
Vln.
2
Vla.
unis.
Cello
unis
pizz.
arco
Bass

95
Fl.
Ob.
Bsn.
Hn.
Hn.
[G♮ D♮]
[C♮]
[B♮ A♮ F♯ G♯]
Pno.
S O L O
Clar.
Vln.
95
1
Vln.
2
pizz.
Vla.
pizz.
Cello
Bass

100
Bng.
one player
S.D.
T.D.
B.D.
snares off
(use S.D. stick)
Pno.
mp secco
105
sf p sub.
stacc.
Vln.
1
2
Vla.
Cello
Bass

Fl.
Ob.
Bsn.
Hn.
Bng.
S.D.
T.D.
B.D.
Hp.
Pno.
marcato
S O L O
Clar.
Vln.
1
Vln.
2
arco
Vla.
Cello
Bass

110
Fl.
Ob.
Bsn.
Hn.
Bng.
S. D.
T. D.
B. D.
Hp.
Pno.
SOLO
Clar.
Vln.
110
1
Vln.
2
Vla.
Cello
Bass

Fl.
Ob.
Bsn.
Hn.
Bng.
Tri.
S.D.
T.D.
B.D.
Vibr.
Hp.
Pno.
SOLO
Clar.
Vln.
Vln.
1
2
Vla.
Cello
Bass
molto
sfz
Solo
ff marc.
mf
ff
[B♭E♭D♭]
f
sub. mf
pizz.

115
Fl.
Ob.
Bsn.
Hn.
Tri.
Vibr.
Hp.
[E♮ D♮]
[A♭]
[A♮ C♯]
Pno.
SOLO
Clar.
Vln.
ff
sub. mf
ff
115
1
Vln.
2
Vla.
Cello
Bass

120
Fl.
Ob.
Bsn.
Hn.
Tri.
Vibr.
Hp.
[A♯]
gliss.
Pno.
SOLO
Clar.
Vln.
sub. mf
120
arco
Vln.
1
2
Vla.
Cello
Bass

Optional
← Repeat
VAR. 3.
Fl.
ff
mp
To Eng. Hn.
Ob.
Bsn.
mp
Hn.
ff
mp
Vibr.
mp
Hp.
mp
[C♭ B♯]
Pno.
mp
S O L O
Clar.
Vln.
Optional
← Repeat
VAR. 3.
pizz.
arco
1
Vln.
2
mp
p
Vla.
Cello
Bass

VARIATION 4
125
Lifeless, Slow (♩=40)
To Piccolo
Fl.
(Eng. Hn.)
E.H.
Bsn.
Hn.
Vibr.
Hp.
[B♮ A♯]
Pno.
SOLO Clar.
SOLO Vln.
VARIATION 4
125
Lifeless, Slow (♩=40)
Vln. 1
Vln. 2
Sola
Vla.
mp espr.
Solo
Cello
Solo, arco
Bass

*Conductor: Everyone (except Piccolo), including soloists, should play a continual glissando between all notes during this variation.

135
Picc.
E. H.
Bsn.
Hn.
Tri.
Gong
Cym.
B.D.
Vibr.
Hp.
[B♭]
[B♮]
Pno.
SOLO
Clar.
Vln.
sock
fff
sfz
p
arco
pizz.
1
Vln.
2
Vla.
Cello
Bass

140
Picc.
molto
E.H.
Bsn.
Hn.
Tri.
Gong
Bng.
S.D.
B.D.
Vibr.
Hp.
Pno.
SOLO
Clar.
Vln.
140
arco
pizz.
arco
1
Vln.
2
Vla.
Cello
arco
pizz.
Bass

145
Picc.
E.H.
Bsn.
Hn.
Tri.
Cym.
S.D.
B.D.
Vibr.
Hp.
Pno.
SOLO
Clar.
Vln.
1
Vln.
2
Vla.
Cello
Bass
rim shot
sock
(loco)
pizz.
arco
fff
sfz
p
pp

150
To Flute
Picc.
E.H.
Bsn.
Hn.
Tri.
Gong
Cym.
B.D.
Vibr.
Hp.
[B♭ D♭ F♭ C♭]
Pno.
SOLO Clar.
SOLO Vln.
150
arco
Vln. 1
Vln. 2
pizz.
Vla.
pizz.
Cello
pizz.
arco
Bass
pizz.
mutes

VARIATION 6
Cold and Strange (in tune) ♩= 60
Fl.
E.H.
Bsn.
Hn.
Solo
mp espr.
Cym.
brush
Vibr.
Hp.
Pno.
SOLO
Clar.
Vln.
VARIATION 6
Cold and Strange (in tune) ♩= 60
Vln. 1
Vln. 2
Vla.
Cello
Bass
mutes
arco

155
Fl.
Flute
pp
E.H.
Bsn.
Hn.
Cym.
Vibr.
Hp.
[C♮ D♮ E♮ F♮ G♭ A♮]
Pno.
(Ped.)
SOLO Clar.
SOLO Vln.
155
Vln. 1
divisi
Vln. 2
Vla.
Cello
Bass

160
Fl.
E.H.
Bsn.
Hn.
pp
Cym.
gliss.
Hp.
ppp
[G♮E♭]
[A♭G♭]
Pno.
To Celesta
(Ped.)
Solo
S O L O
Clar.
p (expressive, but with almost no shading)
Vln.
pppp
160
1
Vln.
2
ppp
Vla.
ppp
div.
Cello
ppp
Bass

165
Fl.
E.H.
Bsn.
Hn.
pp
(pp sempre)
[E♮ A♮]
[G♮E♭]
[A♭G♭]
[G♮ E♮ A♮]
Hp.
Cel.
(Celesta)
pp
S O L O
Clar.
Vln.
p
165
1
Vln.
2
unis.
pp
Vla.
Cello
Bass
(mutes pizz.)

170
Fl.
E.H.
Bsn.
Hn.
Hp.
[E♭ G♭]
[D♭]
[G♮D♮A♭]
[G♭ E♮ A♮]
Cel.
To Piano
SOLO
Clar.
Vln.
170
1
Vln.
2
Vla.
Cello
Bass

175
Flutter
Fl.
E.H.
Bsn.
Hn.
gliss. slowly,
half-valved and fluttertongue
Gong
Vibr.
Hp.
[D♭ F♭]
Pno.
SOLO
Clar.
Vln.
Vln.
Vla.
Cello
trem.
gliss.
Bass
(pizz.)

Fl.
E.H.
Solo
Bsn.
mp
espr.
mf
Hn.
gliss.
gliss.
Gong
Vibr.
Hp.
Pno.
(Ped.)
SOLO
Clar.
Vln.
tr
5
trem.
1
Vln.
2
pp
Vla.
Cello
gliss.
Bass

180
Fl.
E.H.
Bsn.
Hn.
gliss.
put on mute
Gong
Vibr.
Hp.
[F♮ D♮ G♭]
gliss.
Pno.
(Ped.)
S O L O
Clar.
(Solo)
Vln.
180
1 Vln. 2
Vla.
gliss.
Cello
gliss.
Bass

185
rit.
Fl.
E.H.
Bsn.
Hn.
Hp.
[G♮E♭]
[A♭G♭]
[E♮A♮]
Pno.
S O L O
Clar.
pp
Vln.
put on mute
Vln.
1
2
Vla.
Cello
Bass
remove mutes
pp

VARIATION 7

Gently (♩= 69)

VARIATION 8
Fast (𝅗𝅥 = 69)
205
S. D.
muffled
pp
SOLO Clar.
Vln.
(Solo)
ff
senza dim.
flautando
Vla.
pont.
Cello
Bass
210
(ff sempre)
pizz.

215
S. D.
Hp.
S O L O Clar.
Vln.
sempre marcato
1 Vln. 2
Vla.
Cello
Bass
220
225
[F♮ B♮ E♭ A♭]
(pont.)
(pont.)

Fl.
Ob.
Bsn.
Hn.
S. D.
Vibr.
Hp.
Pno.
SOLO Clar.
SOLO Vln.
Vln. 1
Vln. 2
Vla.
Cello
Bass
ord.
(quasi Xylophone)
secco
pizz.
p marc.
(p sempre)

230
flutter
Fl.
Ob.
Bsn.
Hn.
S.D.
Vibr.
Hp.
Pno.
SOLO
Clar.
Vln.
230
1
Vln.
2
Vla.
Cello
Bass

235
Fl.
Ob.
Bsn.
Hn.
S. D.
Vibr.
Hp.
[E♮]
Pno.
SOLO
Clar.
Vln.
235
1
Vln.
2
Vla.
Cello
(pizz.)
Bass

Fl.
Ob.
Bsn.
sfz
Hn.
Gong
sfz
Vibr.
sf
Hp.
mp
[F#]
[G#]
sffz
8
Pno.
sffz
8
SOLO Clar.
ff stridente
SOLO Vln.
Vln. 1
arco
sf
Vln. 2
arco
p marc.
sf
Vla.
Cello
Bass
div. arco
sfz
sfz

240
Fl.
Ob.
Bsn.
mf
Hn.
S. D.
B. D.
f
mf
mf
Hp.
[B♭E♭A♭F♭G♮]
mf
Pno.
mf
SOLO Clar.
SOLO Vln.
mf
(ff sempre)
240
1
Vln.
2
sf
sf
sf
sf
Vla.
mf
Cello
mf
unis.
pizz.
Bass
mf

245
Flutter
Fl.
mf
f
8
Ob.
tr
Bsn.
Hn.
open
S. D.
B. D.
Vibr.
gliss.
Hp.
mp
Pno.
f marc.
S
O
L
O
Clar.
Vln.
245
1
Vln.
2
div.
Vla.
Cello
Bass

Fl.
Ob.
Bsn.
Hn.
S.D.
B.D.
Vibr.
Hp.
Pno.
SOLO
Clar.
Vln.
Vln.
Vla.
Cello
Bass
gliss.
[F♯ C♯ D♯ G♯ B♮ E♮ A♮]

250
Fl.
Ob.
Bsn.
Hn.
gliss.
Bng.
Vibr.
Hp.
Pno.
S
O
L
O
Clar.
Vln.
250
1
Vln.
2
Vla.
pizz.
Cello
arco
Bass

255
Fl.
Ob.
Bsn.
Hn.
Bng.
Vibr.
Hp.
[C♮ G♮ B♭]
Pno.
SOLO Clar.
SOLO Vln.
255
Vln. 1
Vln. 2
Vla.
Cello
Bass

Fl.
Ob.
Bsn.
Hn.
Bng.
S.D.
rim shots
Vibr.
Hp.
[D♮]
Pno.
gliss.
gliss.
S O L O Clar.
(ff sempre)
Vln.
(ff sempre) marcato
div.
1 Vln. 2
Vla.
Cello
arco
Bass

260
Fl.
Ob.
Bsn.
Hn.
Gong
S.D.
Vibr.
Hp.
mp sub.
[F♮ A♭]
Pno.
SOLO
Clar.
Vln.
260
unis.
p poco marc.
div.
Vln. 1
Vln. 2
Vla.
Cello
Bass

265
Fl.
Ob.
Bsn.
Hn.
S.D.
Vibr.
To Glockenspiel
Hp.
Pno.
SOLO
Clar.
Vln.
265
unis.
Vln.
1
2
Vla.
Cello
Bass
mp
f
mf
p

270
Fl.
To Piccolo
Ob.
Bsn.
Hn.
S.D.
Hp.
Pno.
SOLO
Clar.
Vln.
270
Vln.
1
2
pizz.
(non div.)
div.
unis.
arco
mp poco marc.
Vla.
Cello
Bass

275
Picc.
Ob.
ff
Bsn.
ff
Hn.
f
S. D.
ff
Hp.
Pno.
ff
8
S
O
L
O
Clar.
ff
Vln.
275
1
Vln.
2
ff
ff
Vla.
ff
Cello
ff
arco
Bass
ff

280
Piccolo
Picc.
Ob.
Bsn.
Hn.
Hp.
Pno.
(loco)
S O L O
Clar.
Vln.
280
1
Vln.
2
mutes→
Vla.
Cello
Bass

rit.
285
Picc.
Ob.
Solo
ff
f
Bsn.
Solo
f
Hn.
tr
f
p
S.D.
B.D.
ff
sf
Hp.
Pno.
SOLO
Clar.
Vln.
sf
rit.
285
mutes
1
Vln.
2
mutes
tr
mf
pizz.
Vla.
sf
mutes
Cello
ff
mutes
Bass
ff
mutes

VARIATION 9
Calm (♩ = 50)
290
Picc.
mp espr.
Ob.
Bsn.
Solo
mp
Hn.
Glockenspiel or (Celesta)
Glock. (or Cel.)
p
Hp.
p
Pno.
SOLO
Clar.
mp
Vln.
mp
VARIATION 9
Calm (♩ = 50)
290
mutes divisi
tr
1
Vln.
2
p
mutes arco
Vla.
p
divisi mutes
Cello
p
divisi mutes
Bass
p

295
300
Picc.
Ob.
Bsn.
mp
mp
mf
Hn.
Glock.
Hp.
8
Pno.
SOLO
Clar.
Vln.
295
300
(tr♭)
(tr♭)
1
Vln.
2
Vla.
Cello
Bass

Yaddo and New York City
September-December 1966